SPORTS BIOGRAPHIES

JOE BURROW

KENNY ABDO

Fly!
An Imprint of Abdo Zoom
abdobooks.com

abdobooks.com

Published by Abdo Zoom, a division of ABDO, P.O. Box 398166, Minneapolis, Minnesota 55439. Copyright © 2023 by Abdo Consulting Group, Inc. International copyrights reserved in all countries. No part of this book may be reproduced in any form without written permission from the publisher. Fly!™ is a trademark and logo of Abdo Zoom.

Printed in the United States of America, North Mankato, Minnesota.
102022
012023

Photo Credits: Alamy, AP Images, Getty Images, Icon Sportswire, iStock, Shutterstock
Production Contributors: Kenny Abdo, Jennie Forsberg, Grace Hansen
Design Contributors: Neil Klinepier

Library of Congress Control Number: 2022937318

Publisher's Cataloging-in-Publication Data

Names: Abdo, Kenny, author.
Title: Joe Burrow / by Kenny Abdo
Description: Minneapolis, Minnesota : Abdo Zoom, 2023 | Series: Sports biographies | Includes online resources and index.
Identifiers: ISBN 9781098280253 (lib. bdg.) | ISBN 9781098280789 (ebook) | ISBN 9781098281083 (Read-to-Me ebook)
Subjects: LCSH: Burrow, Joe, 1996- --Juvenile literature. | Quarterbacks (Football)--United States--Biography--Juvenile literature. | Cincinnati Bengals (Football team)--Juvenile literature. | American football--Juvenile literature.
Classification: DDC 796.092--dc23

TABLE OF CONTENTS

Joe Burrow...................... 4

Early Years..................... 8

Going Pro...................... 12

Legacy 18

Glossary 22

Online Resources 23

Index 24

JOE BURROW

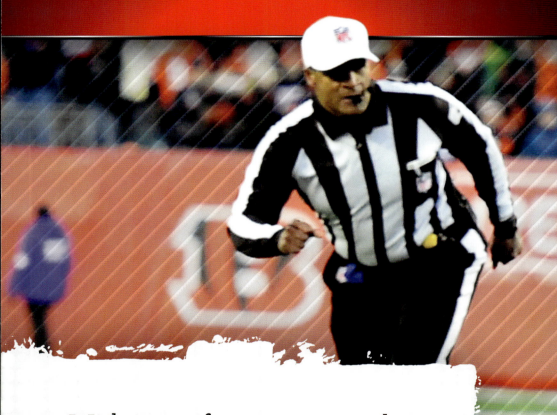

With just a few seasons under his belt, Cincinnati Bengals **quarterback** Joe Burrow is one of the biggest star athletes today!

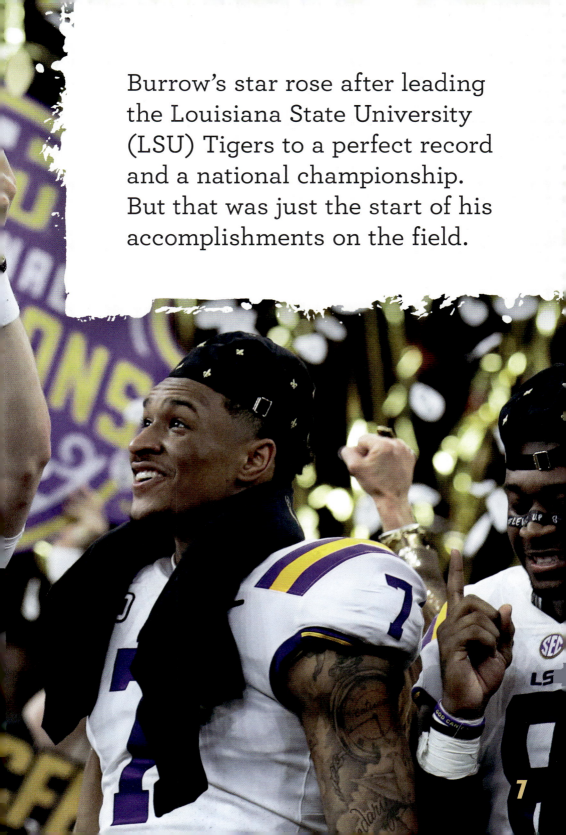

Burrow's star rose after leading the Louisiana State University (LSU) Tigers to a perfect record and a national championship. But that was just the start of his accomplishments on the field.

EARLY YEARS

Joseph Lee Burrow was born in Ames, Iowa, in 1996.

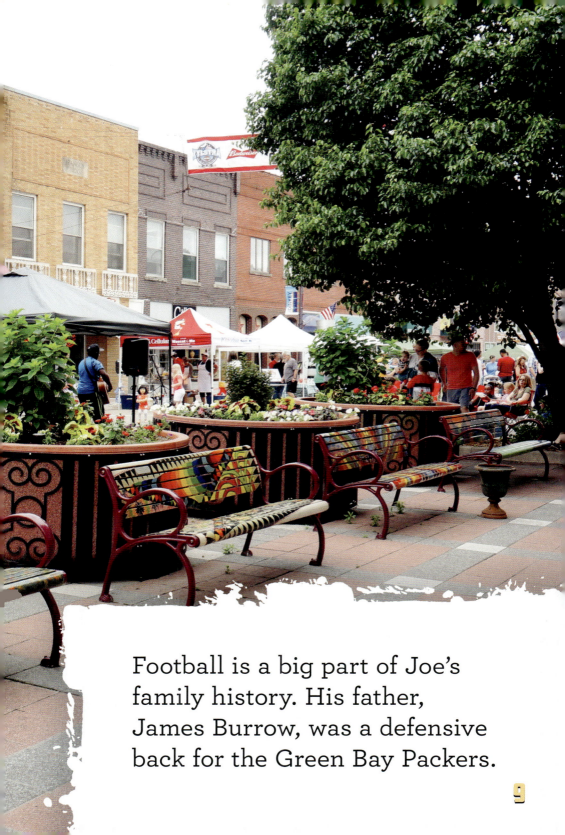

Football is a big part of Joe's family history. His father, James Burrow, was a defensive back for the Green Bay Packers.

The Burrow family moved to Ohio in 2005. Joe played basketball in high school but excelled at football. He took his team to three **playoffs** in a row.

Burrow's college career began at Ohio State in 2014. He spent his last two years of college at LSU. In 2019, he helped the Tigers win the CFP National Championship. Burrow was named offensive **MVP**!

GOING PRO

Burrow was selected by the Cincinnati Bengals in the 2020 NFL **draft**. He was considered a top **quarterback prospect** because of his record-breaking college career.

Burrow broke many NFL records his **rookie** season. He was the first rookie **quarterback** to throw 300-plus yards in three straight games.

In a week 11 game, a hard hit caused a season-ending injury for Burrow. But he worked hard to recover in time for the 2021 season.

Burrow hardly skipped a beat. He and the Bengals worked their way to the 2021 **playoffs**! It was the team's first time back since 1990!

Burrow then led the team to **Super Bowl** LVI. It was the first time the Bengals played in the big game since 1988! The **QB** threw for more than 260 yards and a TD. But it wouldn't be enough to win it all.

LEGACY

Burrow started the Joe Burrow Hunger Relief Fund to support his hometown in Ohio. In high school, Burrow saw people in his community go hungry every day. In 2022, the fund raised 1.5 million dollars!

19

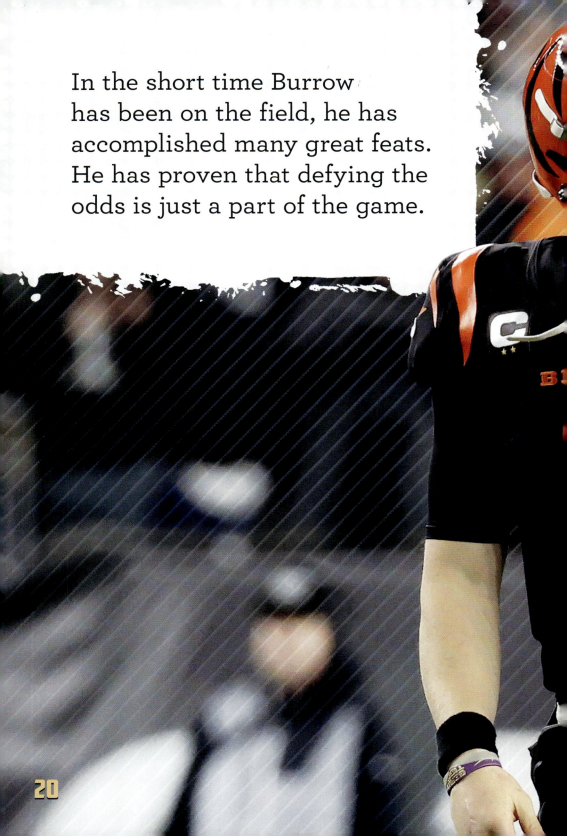

In the short time Burrow has been on the field, he has accomplished many great feats. He has proven that defying the odds is just a part of the game.

GLOSSARY

draft – a process in sports to assign athletes to a certain team.

MVP – short for "most valuable player," an award given in sports to a player who has performed the best in a game or series.

playoffs – a single-elimination tournament held after the regular season to determine the NFL champion.

prospect – a young athlete who is regarded to likely be a great player for a team.

quarterback (QB) – the player on the offensive team that directs teammates in their play.

rookie – a first-year player in a professional sport.

Super Bowl – the NFL championship game, played once a year.

ONLINE RESOURCES

To learn more about Joe Burrow, please visit **abdobooklinks.com** or scan this QR code. These links are routinely monitored and updated to provide the most current information available.

INDEX

Bengals (team) 4, 13

charity 18

family 9, 10

injury 15

Iowa 8

Louisiana State University 7, 11

Ohio 10

Ohio State University 11

Packers (team) 9

records 7, 14

Super Bowl 17